MY
CHRISTMAS
PLANNER

CHRISTMAS 20_____

MY GOALS THIS CHRISTMAS

❖ _____
_____
_____

❖ _____
_____
_____

❖ _____
_____
_____

❖ _____
_____
_____

❖ _____
_____
_____

❖ _____
_____
_____

❖ _____
_____
_____

MONTH

YEAR

Sunday	Monday	Tuesday	Wednesday	Thursday	Friday	Saturday

MONTH

YEAR

Sunday	Monday	Tuesday	Wednesday	Thursday	Friday	Saturday

MONTH

YEAR

Sunday	Monday	Tuesday	Wednesday	Thursday	Friday	Saturday

NOTES:

Christmas To Do List

TO DO	DEADLINE	DONE
Decorate house	November 22	
Christmas Lights	November 22	
Christmas tree	December 8	
Wrap presents	December 23	

Christmas To Do List

TO DO	DEADLINE	DONE

Christmas To Do List

TO DO	DEADLINE	DONE

Christmas To Do List

TO DO	DEADLINE	DONE

Master Gift Shopping List

Name	Detail Page #	Done

Master Gift Shopping List

Name	Detail Page #	Done

Master Gift Shopping List

Name	Detail Page #	Done

Master Gift Shopping List

Name	Detail Page #	Done

Gift Details Page

NAME

_____

_____

Gift Ideas

_____

_____

_____

_____

Gifts Purchased

_____

_____

_____

NAME

_____

_____

Gift Ideas

_____

_____

_____

_____

Gifts Purchased

_____

_____

_____

Gift Details Page

NAME

_____

_____

Gift Ideas

_____

_____

_____

_____

Gifts Purchased

_____

_____

_____

NAME

_____

_____

Gift Ideas

_____

_____

_____

_____

Gifts Purchased

_____

_____

_____

18

Gift Details Page

NAME

_____

_____

Gift Ideas

_____

_____

_____

_____

Gifts Purchased

_____

_____

_____

NAME

_____

_____

Gift Ideas

_____

_____

_____

_____

Gifts Purchased

_____

_____

_____

Gift Details Page

NAME

_____

_____

Gift Ideas

_____

_____

_____

_____

Gifts Purchased

_____

_____

_____

NAME

_____

_____

Gift Ideas

_____

_____

_____

_____

Gifts Purchased

_____

_____

_____

Gift Details Page

NAME

_____

_____

Gift Ideas

_____

_____

_____

_____

Gifts Purchased

_____

_____

_____

NAME

_____

_____

Gift Ideas

_____

_____

_____

_____

Gifts Purchased

_____

_____

_____

Gift Details Page

NAME

_____

_____

Gift Ideas

_____

_____

_____

_____

Gifts Purchased

_____

_____

_____

NAME

_____

_____

Gift Ideas

_____

_____

_____

_____

Gifts Purchased

_____

_____

_____

Gift Details Page

NAME
_____
_____

Gift Ideas
_____
_____
_____
_____

Gifts Purchased
_____
_____
_____

NAME
_____
_____

Gift Ideas
_____
_____
_____
_____

Gifts Purchased
_____
_____
_____

Gift Details Page

NAME

_____

_____

Gift Ideas

_____

_____

_____

_____

Gifts Purchased

_____

_____

_____

NAME

_____

_____

Gift Ideas

_____

_____

_____

_____

Gifts Purchased

_____

_____

_____

Gift Details Page

NAME

_____

_____

Gift Ideas

_____

_____

_____

_____

Gifts Purchased

_____

_____

_____

NAME

_____

_____

Gift Ideas

_____

_____

_____

_____

Gifts Purchased

_____

_____

_____

Gift Details Page

NAME

_____

_____

Gift Ideas

_____

_____

_____

_____

Gifts Purchased

_____

_____

_____

NAME

_____

_____

Gift Ideas

_____

_____

_____

_____

Gifts Purchased

_____

_____

_____

Gift Details Page

NAME

_____

_____

Gift Ideas

_____

_____

_____

_____

Gifts Purchased

_____

_____

_____

NAME

_____

_____

Gift Ideas

_____

_____

_____

_____

Gifts Purchased

_____

_____

_____

Gift Details Page

NAME
_____
_____

Gift Ideas
_____
_____
_____
_____

Gifts Purchased
_____
_____
_____

NAME
_____
_____

Gift Ideas
_____
_____
_____
_____

Gifts Purchased
_____
_____
_____

Gift Details Page

NAME

_____

_____

Gift Ideas

_____

_____

_____

_____

Gifts Purchased

_____

_____

_____

NAME

_____

_____

Gift Ideas

_____

_____

_____

_____

Gifts Purchased

_____

_____

_____

Gift Details Page

NAME

_____

Gift Ideas

_____

_____

_____

_____

Gifts Purchased

_____

_____

_____

NAME

_____

Gift Ideas

_____

_____

_____

_____

Gifts Purchased

_____

_____

_____

Gift Details Page

NAME

_____

_____

Gift Ideas

_____

_____

_____

_____

Gifts Purchased

_____

_____

_____

NAME

_____

_____

Gift Ideas

_____

_____

_____

_____

Gifts Purchased

_____

_____

_____

Gift Details Page

NAME

_____

_____

Gift Ideas

_____

_____

_____

_____

Gifts Purchased

_____

_____

_____

NAME

_____

_____

Gift Ideas

_____

_____

_____

_____

Gifts Purchased

_____

_____

_____

Gift Details Page

NAME

_____

_____

Gift Ideas

_____

_____

_____

_____

Gifts Purchased

_____

_____

_____

NAME

_____

_____

Gift Ideas

_____

_____

_____

_____

Gifts Purchased

_____

_____

_____

Gift Details Page

NAME

_____

_____

Gift Ideas

_____

_____

_____

_____

Gifts Purchased

_____

_____

_____

NAME

_____

_____

Gift Ideas

_____

_____

_____

_____

Gifts Purchased

_____

_____

_____

Gift Details Page

NAME
_____
_____

Gift Ideas
_____
_____
_____
_____

Gifts Purchased
_____
_____
_____

NAME
_____
_____

Gift Ideas
_____
_____
_____
_____

Gifts Purchased
_____
_____
_____

Gift Details Page

NAME

_____

_____

Gift Ideas

_____

_____

_____

_____

Gifts Purchased

_____

_____

_____

NAME

_____

_____

Gift Ideas

_____

_____

_____

_____

Gifts Purchased

_____

_____

_____

Gift Details Page

NAME

_____

_____

Gift Ideas

_____

_____

_____

_____

Gifts Purchased

_____

_____

_____

NAME

_____

_____

Gift Ideas

_____

_____

_____

_____

Gifts Purchased

_____

_____

_____

Christmas Menu

Function:

Starters and Beverages

_____

_____

_____

_____

Main:

_____

_____

_____

_____

Sides:

_____

_____

_____

_____

_____

Dessert:

_____

_____

_____

_____

_____

Christmas Menu

Function:

Starters and Beverages

_____

_____

_____

_____

Main:

_____

_____

_____

_____

Sides:

_____

_____

_____

_____

Dessert:

_____

_____

_____

_____

_____

_____

Christmas Menu

Function:

Starters and Beverages

_____
_____
_____

Main:

_____
_____
_____
_____

Sides:

_____
_____
_____
_____
_____

Dessert:

_____
_____
_____
_____
_____
_____

Christmas Menu

Function:

Starters and Beverages

_____

_____

_____

Main:

_____

_____

_____

_____

Sides:

_____

_____

_____

_____

Dessert:

_____

_____

_____

_____

_____

Christmas Menu

Function:

Starters and Beverages

_____

_____

_____

_____

Main:

_____

_____

_____

_____

_____

Sides:

_____

_____

_____

_____

_____

Dessert:

_____

_____

_____

_____

_____

_____

Grocery List

Function:	Date:

Grocery List

Function: Date:

_____   _____

_____   _____

_____   _____

_____   _____

_____   _____

_____   _____

_____   _____

_____   _____

_____   _____

_____   _____

_____   _____

_____   _____

_____   _____

_____   _____

_____   _____

_____   _____

_____   _____

_____   _____

_____   _____

_____   _____

_____   _____

_____   _____

Grocery List

Function:	Date:

_____   _____
_____   _____
_____   _____
_____   _____
_____   _____
_____   _____
_____   _____
_____   _____
_____   _____
_____   _____
_____   _____
_____   _____
_____   _____
_____   _____
_____   _____
_____   _____
_____   _____
_____   _____
_____   _____
_____   _____
_____   _____
_____   _____

Grocery List

Function: _____   Date: _____

_____	_____
_____	_____
_____	_____
_____	_____
_____	_____
_____	_____
_____	_____
_____	_____
_____	_____
_____	_____
_____	_____
_____	_____
_____	_____
_____	_____
_____	_____
_____	_____
_____	_____
_____	_____
_____	_____
_____	_____
_____	_____
_____	_____
_____	_____
_____	_____

Grocery List

Function:	Date:

_____   _____

_____   _____

_____   _____

_____   _____

_____   _____

_____   _____

_____   _____

_____   _____

_____   _____

_____   _____

_____   _____

_____   _____

_____   _____

_____   _____

_____   _____

_____   _____

_____   _____

_____   _____

_____   _____

_____   _____

_____   _____

_____   _____

CHRISTMAS MEMORIES

YEAR: PLACE:

SHARED WITH:

_____
_____
_____
_____
_____
_____
_____

FAVORITE MOMENTS

_____
_____
_____
_____
_____
_____
_____
_____
_____
_____
_____
_____
_____

CHRISTMAS MEMORIES

YEAR: PLACE:

SHARED WITH:

_____
_____
_____
_____
_____
_____
_____

FAVORITE MOMENTS

_____
_____
_____
_____
_____
_____
_____
_____
_____
_____
_____
_____
_____

CHRISTMAS MEMORIES

YEAR: PLACE:

SHARED WITH:

_____

_____

_____

_____

_____

_____

_____

FAVORITE MOMENTS

_____

_____

_____

_____

_____

_____

_____

_____

_____

_____

_____

_____

_____

CHRISTMAS MEMORIES

YEAR: PLACE:

SHARED WITH:

_____

_____

_____

_____

_____

_____

_____

FAVORITE MOMENTS

_____

_____

_____

_____

_____

_____

_____

_____

_____

_____

_____

_____

_____

_____

Christmas Mailing Addresses

Name:

Address:

Name:

Address:

Name:

Address:

Name:

Address:

Name:

Address:

Christmas Mailing Addresses

Name:

Address:

Name:

Address:

Name:

Address:

Name:

Address:

Name:

Address:

Christmas Mailing Addresses

Name:

Address:

Name:

Address:

Name:

Address:

Name:

Address:

Name:

Address:

Christmas Mailing Addresses

Name:

Address:

Name:

Address:

Name:

Address:

Name:

Address:

Name:

Address:

Christmas Mailing Addresses

Name:

Address:

Name:

Address:

Name:

Address:

Name:

Address:

Name:

Address:

NOTES:

NOTES:

NOTES:

NOTES:

NOTES:

NOTES:

CHRISTMAS 20_____

MY GOALS THIS CHRISTMAS

❖ _____
_____
_____

❖ _____
_____
_____

❖ _____
_____
_____

❖ _____
_____
_____

❖ _____
_____
_____

❖ _____
_____
_____

❖ _____
_____
_____

MONTH

YEAR

Sunday	Monday	Tuesday	Wednesday	Thursday	Friday	Saturday

MONTH

YEAR

Sunday	Monday	Tuesday	Wednesday	Thursday	Friday	Saturday

MONTH

YEAR

Sunday	Monday	Tuesday	Wednesday	Thursday	Friday	Saturday

NOTES:

Christmas To Do List

TO DO	DEADLINE	DONE

Christmas To Do List

TO DO	DEADLINE	DONE

Christmas To Do List

TO DO	DEADLINE	DONE

Christmas To Do List

TO DO	DEADLINE	DONE

Master Gift Shopping List

Name	Detail Page #	Done

Master Gift Shopping List

Name	Detail Page #	Done

Master Gift Shopping List

Name	Detail Page #	Done

Master Gift Shopping List

Name	Detail Page #	Done

Gift Details Page

NAME

_____

_____

Gift Ideas

_____

_____

_____

_____

Gifts Purchased

_____

_____

_____

NAME

_____

_____

Gift Ideas

_____

_____

_____

_____

Gifts Purchased

_____

_____

_____

Gift Details Page

NAME

_____

_____

Gift Ideas

_____

_____

_____

_____

Gifts Purchased

_____

_____

_____

NAME

_____

_____

Gift Ideas

_____

_____

_____

_____

Gifts Purchased

_____

_____

_____

Gift Details Page

NAME

_____

_____

Gift Ideas

_____

_____

_____

_____

Gifts Purchased

_____

_____

_____

NAME

_____

_____

Gift Ideas

_____

_____

_____

_____

Gifts Purchased

_____

_____

_____

Gift Details Page

NAME

_____

_____

Gift Ideas

_____

_____

_____

_____

Gifts Purchased

_____

_____

_____

NAME

_____

_____

Gift Ideas

_____

_____

_____

_____

Gifts Purchased

_____

_____

_____

Gift Details Page

NAME

_____

_____

Gift Ideas

_____

_____

_____

_____

Gifts Purchased

_____

_____

_____

NAME

_____

_____

Gift Ideas

_____

_____

_____

_____

Gifts Purchased

_____

_____

_____

Gift Details Page

NAME

_____

_____

Gift Ideas

_____

_____

_____

Gifts Purchased

_____

_____

_____

NAME

_____

_____

Gift Ideas

_____

_____

_____

Gifts Purchased

_____

_____

_____

Gift Details Page

NAME

_____

_____

Gift Ideas

_____

_____

_____

_____

Gifts Purchased

_____

_____

_____

NAME

_____

_____

Gift Ideas

_____

_____

_____

_____

Gifts Purchased

_____

_____

_____

Gift Details Page

NAME

_____

_____

Gift Ideas

_____

_____

_____

_____

Gifts Purchased

_____

_____

_____

NAME

_____

_____

Gift Ideas

_____

_____

_____

_____

Gifts Purchased

_____

_____

_____

Gift Details Page

NAME

_____

_____

Gift Ideas

_____

_____

_____

_____

Gifts Purchased

_____

_____

_____

NAME

_____

_____

Gift Ideas

_____

_____

_____

_____

Gifts Purchased

_____

_____

_____

Gift Details Page

NAME

_____

_____

Gift Ideas

_____

_____

_____

_____

Gifts Purchased

_____

_____

_____

NAME

_____

_____

Gift Ideas

_____

_____

_____

_____

Gifts Purchased

_____

_____

_____

Gift Details Page

NAME

_____

_____

Gift Ideas

_____

_____

_____

_____

Gifts Purchased

_____

_____

_____

NAME

_____

_____

Gift Ideas

_____

_____

_____

_____

Gifts Purchased

_____

_____

_____

Gift Details Page

NAME

_____

_____

Gift Ideas

_____

_____

_____

_____

Gifts Purchased

_____

_____

_____

NAME

_____

_____

Gift Ideas

_____

_____

_____

_____

Gifts Purchased

_____

_____

_____

Gift Details Page

NAME

_____

_____

Gift Ideas

_____

_____

_____

_____

Gifts Purchased

_____

_____

_____

NAME

_____

_____

Gift Ideas

_____

_____

_____

_____

Gifts Purchased

_____

_____

_____

Gift Details Page

NAME

_____

_____

Gift Ideas

_____

_____

_____

_____

Gifts Purchased

_____

_____

_____

NAME

_____

_____

Gift Ideas

_____

_____

_____

_____

Gifts Purchased

_____

_____

_____

Gift Details Page

NAME

_____

_____

Gift Ideas

_____

_____

_____

_____

Gifts Purchased

_____

_____

_____

NAME

_____

_____

Gift Ideas

_____

_____

_____

_____

Gifts Purchased

_____

_____

_____

Gift Details Page

NAME
_____
_____

Gift Ideas
_____
_____
_____
_____

Gifts Purchased
_____
_____
_____

NAME
_____
_____

Gift Ideas
_____
_____
_____
_____

Gifts Purchased
_____
_____
_____

Gift Details Page

NAME

_____

_____

Gift Ideas

_____

_____

_____

_____

Gifts Purchased

_____

_____

_____

NAME

_____

_____

Gift Ideas

_____

_____

_____

_____

Gifts Purchased

_____

_____

_____

Gift Details Page

NAME

_____

_____

Gift Ideas

_____

_____

_____

_____

Gifts Purchased

_____

_____

_____

NAME

_____

_____

Gift Ideas

_____

_____

_____

_____

Gifts Purchased

_____

_____

_____

Gift Details Page

NAME

_____

_____

Gift Ideas

_____

_____

_____

_____

Gifts Purchased

_____

_____

_____

NAME

_____

_____

Gift Ideas

_____

_____

_____

_____

Gifts Purchased

_____

_____

_____

Gift Details Page

NAME

_____

_____

Gift Ideas

_____

_____

_____

_____

Gifts Purchased

_____

_____

_____

NAME

_____

_____

Gift Ideas

_____

_____

_____

_____

Gifts Purchased

_____

_____

_____

Gift Details Page

NAME

_____

_____

Gift Ideas

_____

_____

_____

_____

Gifts Purchased

_____

_____

_____

NAME

_____

_____

Gift Ideas

_____

_____

_____

_____

Gifts Purchased

_____

_____

_____

Christmas Menu

Function:

Starters and Beverages

_____

_____

_____

Main:

_____

_____

_____

_____

Sides:

_____

_____

_____

_____

Dessert:

_____

_____

_____

_____

_____

_____

Christmas Menu

Function:

Starters and Beverages

_____

_____

_____

_____

Main:

_____

_____

_____

_____

Sides:

_____

_____

_____

_____

_____

Dessert:

_____

_____

_____

_____

_____

_____

Christmas Menu

Function:

Starters and Beverages

_____

_____

_____

_____

Main:

_____

_____

_____

_____

Sides:

_____

_____

_____

_____

_____

Dessert:

_____

_____

_____

_____

_____

_____

Christmas Menu

Function:

Starters and Beverages

_____

_____

_____

_____

Main:

_____

_____

_____

_____

Sides:

_____

_____

_____

_____

_____

Dessert:

_____

_____

_____

_____

_____

_____

Christmas Menu

Function:

Starters and Beverages

_____

_____

_____

_____

Main:

_____

_____

_____

_____

Sides:

_____

_____

_____

_____

Dessert:

_____

_____

_____

_____

_____

Grocery List

Function:	Date:

_____   _____
_____   _____
_____   _____
_____   _____
_____   _____
_____   _____
_____   _____
_____   _____
_____   _____
_____   _____
_____   _____
_____   _____
_____   _____
_____   _____
_____   _____
_____   _____
_____   _____
_____   _____
_____   _____
_____   _____
_____   _____

Grocery List

Function:	Date:

Grocery List

Function: Date:

_____   _____
_____   _____
_____   _____
_____   _____
_____   _____
_____   _____
_____   _____
_____   _____
_____   _____
_____   _____
_____   _____
_____   _____
_____   _____
_____   _____
_____   _____
_____   _____
_____   _____
_____   _____
_____   _____
_____   _____
_____   _____
_____   _____

Grocery List

Function:	Date:

_____   _____

_____   _____

_____   _____

_____   _____

_____   _____

_____   _____

_____   _____

_____   _____

_____   _____

_____   _____

_____   _____

_____   _____

_____   _____

_____   _____

_____   _____

_____   _____

_____   _____

_____   _____

_____   _____

_____   _____

_____   _____

_____   _____

_____   _____

_____   _____

Grocery List

Function:	Date:

_____   _____
_____   _____
_____   _____
_____   _____
_____   _____
_____   _____
_____   _____
_____   _____
_____   _____
_____   _____
_____   _____
_____   _____
_____   _____
_____   _____
_____   _____
_____   _____
_____   _____
_____   _____
_____   _____
_____   _____
_____   _____

CHRISTMAS MEMORIES

YEAR: PLACE:

SHARED WITH:

_____

_____

_____

_____

_____

_____

_____

FAVORITE MOMENTS

_____

_____

_____

_____

_____

_____

_____

_____

_____

_____

_____

_____

_____

_____

CHRISTMAS MEMORIES

YEAR: PLACE:

SHARED WITH:

_____

_____

_____

_____

_____

_____

_____

FAVORITE MOMENTS

_____

_____

_____

_____

_____

_____

_____

_____

_____

_____

_____

_____

_____

CHRISTMAS MEMORIES

YEAR: PLACE:

SHARED WITH:

_____

_____

_____

_____

_____

_____

_____

FAVORITE MOMENTS

_____

_____

_____

_____

_____

_____

_____

_____

_____

_____

_____

_____

_____

CHRISTMAS MEMORIES

YEAR: PLACE:

SHARED WITH:

_____

_____

_____

_____

_____

_____

_____

FAVORITE MOMENTS

_____

_____

_____

_____

_____

_____

_____

_____

_____

_____

_____

_____

Christmas Mailing Addresses

Name:

Address:

Name:

Address:

Name:

Address:

Name:

Address:

Name:

Address:

Christmas Mailing Addresses

Name:

Address:

Name:

Address:

Name:

Address:

Name:

Address:

Name:

Address:

Christmas Mailing Addresses

Name:

Address:

Name:

Address:

Name:

Address:

Name:

Address:

Name:

Address:

Christmas Mailing Addresses

Name:

Address:

Name:

Address:

Name:

Address:

Name:

Address:

Name:

Address:

Christmas Mailing Addresses

Name:

Address:

Name:

Address:

Name:

Address:

Name:

Address:

Name:

Address:

NOTES:

NOTES:

NOTES:

NOTES:

NOTES:

NOTES:

89643144R00071

Made in the USA
San Bernardino, CA
28 September 2018